CO-AJW-053
3 2711 00178 7252

JAN 1 9 2010

Philip Fried, a New York-based poet and little-magazine editor, has published three previous books of poetry: *Mutual Trespasses* (1988); *Quantum Genesis* (1997), which A.R. Ammons called "a major new testament"; and *Big Men Speaking to Little Men* (Salmon, 2006), which—said Marilyn Hacker— "represents much of what I admire in contemporary American poetry...." Fried also collaborated with his wife, the fine-art photographer Lynn Saville, on a volume combining her nocturnal photographs with poetry from around the world. And he is the founder of *The Manhattan Review*, an international journal that for three decades has published the best in Anglophone poetry and translations.

Cohort

ALSO BY PHILIP FRIED

Mutual Trespasses

Quantum Genesis

Big Men Speaking to Little Men

Acquainted With The Night
(With Lynn Saville), Editor

Columbia College Library
600 South Michigan
Chicago, IL 60605

Cohort
Philip Fried

salmonpoetry

Published in 2009 by
Salmon Poetry,
Cliffs of Moher, County Clare, Ireland
Website: www.salmonpoetry.com
Email: info@salmonpoetry.com

Copyright © Philip Fried 2009

ISBN 978-0-9561287-0-6

All rights reserved. No part of this publication may be reproduced or transmitted in any form or by any means, electronic or mechanical, including photography, recording, or any information storage or retrieval system, without permission in writing from the publisher. The book is sold subject to the condition that it shall not, by way of trade or otherwise, be lent, resold or otherwise circulated without the publisher's prior consent in any form of binding or cover other than that in which it is published and without a similar condition, including this condition, being imposed on the subsequent purchaser.

Cover photography: 'Intersection' by Lynn Saville
Typesetting: Patrick Chapman
Cover Design: Siobhán Hutson

For Lynn, with all my love

Acknowledgements

"Minuet"
"Interface"   BARROW STREET

"Reversible Swirl"
"A Mind of Summer"
"Sealed Warrant"   NTHPOSITION

"Dear Auditor"   POET LORE

"Advice to the Gods"
"The Oral Tradition"
"Operation Countdown"   STIMULUS RESPOND

"Short Line Driver
(in the Garden State)"   TERRAIN.ORG

"Short Line Driver (in the Garden State)" nominated by
Terrain.org for Best of the Net, 2006.

"Reversible Swirl" chosen for *Nthposition* anthology.

Contents

REVERSIBLE SWIRL

Short Line Driver
(in the Garden State)

Not God but the lead-footed, combustible
bus-driver steers our destinies—
no appeals except to the wheel.
So bouncing in potholes, no matter the wobble
in the spin, the wandering poles, the rifting
plates, we ply our cosmic commute,

with *her* keen eye in the rear-view mirror
to check out reckless comets, ensure
we leave no litter, just a molecular
flurry, little stuff, when we leave.
Her uniform, custom designed by the Line,
features gilded cuffs and crescent-

moon-shaped epaulets like scythes
at the shoulders; it's a pleasure to wake
each humdrum day to find her driving
us to work, but what a temper:
the chatter of billions, stuffed with banality's
weightless luggage, drives her crazy.

Good thing there's a fraternity
of drivers, the jocular shock-absorbers,
kidding on two-way radios
about asteroid traffic, mocking the daily
fool, some soul at the bus-stop
confusing your local run with the time-

warp express to the end of it all.
She smirks, they all do, at this poor
petitioner who appears at her soon-
to-be-shut door, smirks from the official

condescending height of her gritty
weather-streaked vehicle and croons,

"Honey, it's coming in twenty, just
hang on." Petty sadism, yes, but
who else will speak for combustion, exhaust
gases, thermal cycles, imperfect
reactions, inevitable losses,
residue? Who else will get us through?

Advice to the Gods

I am a consigliere to the gods
of travel, but they rarely consult me, the journey
through all the late hours is interminable, we are always
between cities, behind our Cyclopean headlight.
No longer do we travel from car to car.

I recall my masters stowing bulky coats
on overhead racks. Now every left wrist is adorned
with a chain that snakes to a slim portfolio,
gear for couriers in this expanding
stain of indelible lateness. We are poised

to arrive in the greatest city of all. But the gods
are losing interest in astonishment's drama.
Now that the world is derelict and humans
have fled like refugees into the well mouth
to discover an older, pre-Aztec water,

the glistening morning of organized river valleys,
a few realize that eons ago a glitter
of quartz in the pavement should have been scried, a weed
or a soda cap should have been interrogated.
But this very minute it is too late and the train

zooms at zero altitude through family
backyards, whooshing by mowers and pools, reducing
all that it passes to less of a place, too close,
more and more local. Sometime soon, the gods
will begin to rise, to smell their own sour breath.

I am brimming with advice for them—it won't
be followed. Masters, whatever you do, be sure
of the scale of your arrival, you may have become
incongruous with the story itself, worship
won't find you, who are now too large or too little.

Reversible Swirl

The grill cloth on our Zenith Tombstone
displayed the reversible swirl pattern.
Clay-color, it emitted heat
like a potter's kiln that was baking vibrations.

The swirls leaped like dolphins sporting
in fabled seas, like the voices themselves:
Jamaica, Maui, Tasmania...
meanings faint, accents abounding.

Evenings I knelt at that hearth and altar,
grandpa, grandma, mom, dad, arrayed
behind me, the ceramic family
whose chatter cooled to the overglaze.

The pulsing grill cloth was the screen
I bowed to, intent, my shadow-self leaning
right through to the tabernacle of tubes,
into the filaments' holy of holies,

appraising ionic disturbances,
my face the glowing dial, tuning
the globe as solar flares allowed.
The late war had defeated history,

now we lived in the pleroma
of voices, signals, it was all radio.
At night the bedsprings picked up transmissions
that were bending around the edge of the future.

THE ORAL TRADITION

Cohort

1. time-lapse photography

the Big Bang is the starter's gun
war's over and the universe
springs from a void that seethes with nothing

new-born time is populous
with seconds jostling round the clock
convertibles bassinets playpens cribs

from sperm in shoals to minnow in schools
identical desks with inkwell holes
pointers in unison point at the rules

in time-lapse photography flowers bloom
fruit rots and men commute to the city
shelves empty re-fill with units of product

i too am an early or late bloomer
with rank in the family a budding consumer

2. an ink dot speaks

first i was only an ignorant dot
iota in the countless cohort
unique and yet only a part

equally of victim and killer
victory parade or surrender
oh how eyes devoured ignored

me but i returned the gaze
lost in the day's face the crisp
leader bound for a yellowing limbo

litany of casualties
but all the time it was i crying
in folds of the paper the comforter

then a breeze out of oblivion
tickled the fire's quick ambition

3. the body's cohort

self in a crowd was a crowd in itself
upraised arm crying teacher i know
in eager dumb-show but underarm

mulling over its odor of me
stirred up in a drill of side-straddle-hop
then drowned in the gym's big alphabet soup

mouth straining to speak and corrected for chatter
hand that bears an anointed note
through the dim corridors of permission

knee that is cautioned not to obstruct
feet commanded by bell to dismissal
knuckle that tries to rub out the mote

which flicked into the socketed eye
and might be the seed of Ygdrasil.

The Oral Tradition

Once I woke from blackout into a later
now, a voice explaining like a calm
adult to the frightened child I was
that nothing really bad had happened, *nothing
happened to you, and it's not bad*, filling in gaps,
saying, *not accident*, and telling a story
about a time when something usual happened
and someone didn't go away. *I go on talking*

as if you were listening. I'm the per diem griot,
bard of the humdrum, right foot after left,
but sometimes you step off into falls and forgetting,
vacations in the time before narrative,
and I search out a motif, to mend the story
that holds the world together by word of mouth.

Operation Countdown

Piercing the heaven of the amnion,
staticky voices foretell the end of the War,
while my embryo rehearses amphibian landings
and in leisure moments peruses the *Elements*
of Euclid, right-angled tome that takes in the seas
and every drowning. My fetus semaphores
bipedal and *Homo habilis*. Even the slant rhyme
voice and *loss* comes true in the Pleistocene.

No man's land—I'm inching through the barbed wire
of the First Great War on the cratered path to the Second...
birth and bombardment, shrapnel of self that is lodged,
poor infantry, in the flesh of a godawful howl.
Then all the voices broadcast again in the mobile
of teeth and lips, cheek with a stubble of static—

A Mind of Summer

Nothing moment, empty, outside the zone
of lockers, on the mica-inflected pavement,
opaque and glittering, that leads to the pool.
Inside that mini-city of undressing,
dressing, even old paint is peeling off
the Dutch doors of the doll-like changing houses,
while squirts of chatter, cries, and laughter butter
the air like coconut-lotion. This is the sanctum

of excited transition. But showered, dressed, I'm waiting
between these changes and the day that is broken
into diamonds by the cyclone fence.
Butt perched on a wall that warms my calves, I'm leaning
back against the springy metal, open
at last to the eroded dominions of Nothing...

Sealed Warrant

In a single night the crystals of silence have fallen,
by dawn forming the walls of buildings and gardens,
everything settled into a world, as a few
stick figures are the stragglers or the vanguard,
parading dabs of color in the narrow
strip between hats and scribbled shadows. All
is overshadowed by the wall that stands
and runs to a turning. You are the material

witness implicated by every window,
invisible although your forehead is known
to conceal a noisy silence in any street.
With this sealed warrant, entered on the docket,
I hereby name you, who shall go nameless,
and detain you in a limbo of secrecy.

The Endless Pool ®

Soon we'll all be given little treadmill
oceans like this one, where we can slip out of time
and into the endless moment, to overcome glitches
like foot-drag and the tendency to veer
off-line. (Use a pull-buoy for these issues.)
Exercising our metaphysical-mind-
muscle by picturing, somewhere ahead, the fist
of an engine churning up time from no-time,

sending the flow back through the present into
the past that begins with the kick. The endless complaining
dead reduced at last to a tickle of wavelets
on ribs. Their anonymous, abetting chorus
intoning, *the future sustains your every stroke,*
history is fitful foam that bursts at your heels.

"By Babylon's flow-charts..."

By Babylon's flow-charts I sat down and wept, far
from home, my player-piano hands still appeasing
data-gods with the ragtime of input, clicks
and bits. Signed A. Corpuscle, Manager,
my reports were forwarded through the veins of Marduk,
who thrashes in sleep, his dreams re-structuring
the set-up, re-jiggering the divvy of tribute.
And we, we were a swarm intelligence. *Get it?*

Got it!—twitching down our pheromone lanes...
My little dream? Somewhere ages and ages hence,
you in Zion will read this lamentation
cached among the priestly protocols,
you whose eyes are only an augury,
a diviner's inkling from the faulty entrails.

Cousin Henry

Unglued! Henry's black beret, café
icon, flew off one windy life—instantly
replaced by a mane of salt-peppery hair. Henry
the Philosopher re-aligning as Henry the Chemist.
Hatless in his trim garage, he mixed
fanatic adhesives to be shipped via
a middleman Puerto Rican to Arabs: Díaz,
Abu Dhabi, the names that only a one-man

Jew could fasten together. His inventory:
ironies like wrenches of all sizes
aligned on hooks above the engineless space
and ancient but elegant tools like the Spinoza,
designed to cohere the world with theorems,
to solder man and God to Necessity.

Motions in the Court of Final Appeal

We could not stop for death. We took a limo.
In which Izzy, a Brooklyn lawyer, told me, "Never
point at a judge. Say, 'your honor, may I
offer a motion.'" And moving in rows, we remembered
a son who buried his father transitively
in the passive voice: debts paid and choices made.
We were traveling in this ample confined space,
it was uncertain how far, to where a hole

dropped, not far, in the bottomless well of time.
To where gravediggers, in our frame of haste,
would lean patiently on a stone for the ceremony.
And where many hands would dangle while an obsessive
shoveler pointed the unwieldy ceremonial
tool again and again in an offer of proof.

Ghost Army

The soft-spoken lyric revels in D–Day deceptions:
aural gears of invisible half-tracks and trucks
roughhouse the air in plain daylight. At midnight
the full moon surveils rows of inflatable tanks.
Cached at the heart of the secret, a lone GI,
not even a sentinel, far from the picket line
where pseudo-battalions are roiling at the edges...
Or maybe needing to live the war I never

fought, I myself am the ghost army. The signals
a large force would send in mobilizing
are my small talk, my half-coded requisitions.
Each morning before the mirror, the ego's accoutered
for the phony invasion of the Pas-de-Calais...
It's the working stiff who's a figment of radar deceptions.

Identity Theft

Reader, good citizen, watch as I pickpocket
my own ID, to impersonate myself
on paper. Home in on the waltz of mark and dip,
with distraction's music wheezed out by the stall,
as the score, lifted, glides from shot to drop.
To cop—yes me, I'll step in to make the collar,
and relying on your witness report, indict
myself. Case closed. No, that's when true crime begins—

From behind high-tensile steel bars, I can deploy
dumpster-divers to ransack for bits of self,
shoulder-surfers to nab every skein of code,
phishers to spoof a PayPal account. I'll commit
frauds in Philip Fried's name. I'll be victim, cloned
identities, grifter ... You be the faceless witness.

Thesaurus rex

Dog-eared carnivore and gormandizer
of libraries, it's come to this, alas—
mere shattered maxilla of a primitive form
dating from the Jurassic before the loss
of declamation (not one equivalent, Yorick?).
Today just a few slivers, *Colloq.* or *Ant.*,
shards of boards, a faint synonym odor
to conjure the flesh of words, a million dinners

fueling dreams of *power puissance dominion
might omnipotence*, with only a hint
—in re *quarry* or *sheep*—of *meekness submission*...
But now in pastures new, thesaurus.com,
a gamboling raptor, restores the pastoral fantasy:
sway control almightiness potency.

Tech Help

Words began at the mind's fingers, flakes
of flint we knapped and traded. But we flourished
in the weather of voices as the heavens rained
divinity into our cortical folds. Thunder
organized wars, allocated the booty
and crops. Or in caves a silty larynx ordained
the flooding river's predictability...
Our well-groomed voices broadcast news and weather:

low-pressure systems moving in and body
counts, while the treble, feedback-troubled PA
crackles *pray* or sputters *evacuate*.
And Tech Help soothes the ear, an outsourced voice
dosing the delusion of *why* with *how*
as it coaches the mind's fingers through their confusion.

Scratching Nightingale

Found your vintage Nightingale in a thrift
shop, your well-warped 78 that croons
so mellow *hear each other groan* in treble.
But *half in love with easeful* spins too soon
from *dim* to *blown* to *foam of perilous*,
so I need to make the needle skip, re-groove,
make your nightingale tweak, chirp, and scribble.
Saying tough little motherless son of a bitch is no dis-

respect, I mean to plunder your hoard of loss...
My dear dad, loving Presence, owned the absence
of Pinza on vinyl in *Faust*: oh what a voice—
in a puff of smoke, a handsome devil, *Voici!*
My father's dominion was scattered, *a few, sad, last*
epiphanies peeking from dog-eared record sleeves.

Born Again

Say I was born of language, with my name
wedged against other names, an accommodation
on paper, but she also registered me
in the Hotel of the Real, a one-room suite,
checking me in with my light baggage of guts,
of organs, of blood, accessory kit of nerves.
Later, I signaled her in semaphore,
with hands as flags, "adrift … emergency."

Then, say I was born to live in a welter of rooms,
many more than there were, in each a bystander
gawking at the accident of me
run aground on a threshold, wrecked in my games—
until summoned by the dried pulp of paper,
its fibrous sigh easing a graphite glide.

Shifty Tent

Penned in this narrow bed I am bundled in
with my selves (and you?) like siblings feet to head
to feet—and drowned by a soft sky, who can count
smelly toes or gritted teeth and tell whose
or know how resentments breed in this shifty tent?
When mother tucking us in would dole out
one story that told of a single victory,
some of us wondered about the bad elder brothers

and fell asleep unanswered. A wolf's belly,
our bed gives birth to a litter every morning
whose appetites go unappeased by cereal.
Cynical about stories, we crowd into
encounters, jeering (at you?), *If you're a fairy-tale*
helper with many friends, sort out our too many selves.

Inchmeal: A Sermon

Pulsing, radiating cities provide
long perspectives, vistas like odysseys
of the eyes, which even after the body turns
away, pursue impossible horizons.
Even my briefest glances have abandoned
me, prodigals who returned even younger,
as in St. Einstein's parable of the twins.
The moral: Our least wish is a whole other

life—who can make a meal of the incremental?
So, brother, sister, give your hands over to bric-
a-brac repairs of the possible, allow
your fingers to tinker and be cobbled into
little bone-houses for birds, a doll's gazebo,
but loose your ragged glances to journey and beg...

Before the Final Assault

Tenting on this 6-foot ledge, with Everest's
peak, if it even exists—apex where Up
will plummet—lost in night, we're canted at 30
degrees to the face of language. This morning, roped
in thought to our goal, with its counted-off altitude,
I felt the crust of words give way, I slid
backward before regaining a hold and found,
looking between my legs, a 10,000-

foot drop into the boundless snow glare of paper.
Reader, masked and wool-shrouded companion,
we're all alone on this final assault, forget
the 350 porters of tradition,
the tons of food at the base. In tomorrow's never,
inchmeal, we devour the icy promise.

Son Net

Nameless dark lady, you've made me into your zombie.
I set up the motherboard circuits for these sonnets
to bemoan the she who goads me to oxymoron—
it was only an invitation to your botnets.
Now you're cashing in on my bandwidth currency
to spew your spam love letters to the markets,
committing click-fraud, phishing, recruiting money
mules, making me an unwitting dupe of your vectors.

My life online is guided by you, remotely,
my immortal fame, your trashing of my anonymous
name, probably from a suburb of Kenosha.
Lady, the soul that peeks from the words of lovers
is only your means for transmitting a code that's malicious.
We're all just knots on your cyber-"cat," Ms. Rimbaud.

Minuet

Silent howl. Cut-out, iridescent, metallic
coyote. Outcast, I've earned a suburban niche,
parked on the corporate lawn like a stalking predator.
Facsimile *Canis latrans* to scare the *Branta*

nonmigratus. Wildlife's a bit awry
when fat-cat geese disdain their ancestral fly-
ways, v-shaped honks resounding above your routes
as they sleekly pursue only their local commutes.

I want to report—but to whom?—a transmutation
as gravely two by two in a minuet
web feet and wing-tips are exchanging positions:
folks waddling, birds with bifocals like cosseted pets

staring vexed at paper so wordy and grainless
with a sporadic peck at a period. Fruitless.

Interface

Laptop riding a lap on the bus. Across
the screen some trees are gliding, irrelevant
scenery, a sliding less-than-surface,
while the protocol bids us to remain intent

and be what we're becoming: fingers, a face.
Two circuits, digital and neuronal, mirror
and tease each other out of depth, like Monet's
water-lilies, floating, drifting, where?

Pond or nebula? So, we meet here...
A bit nostalgic for the punched-card phase,
the data of oxymorons hammered by keys
in stiff cardstock, sick health and freezing fire,

but committed to the empty you I've shaped
to hover over the fluent interface.

Voir Dire

Fellow-juror, I'm ready to confess,
wheedle, coax, suborn, and throw myself
on the mercy of the court or any passerby
just when they've asked us to forswear all bias.

Is the judge really named Libel? Did his gavel say,
"How many histories we can sift in this case,
in which the state, defendant, and star witness
are one, and how many cases in this history..."?

Were these the words of McFluke, assistant d.a.?—
"Tell us the state of mind in which you reside,
victim or criminal. At each stage of this case,
you must interject what you want most to hide."

Compadre in justice, let's rise and without a defense,
swear, "Wood-paneled allegory, strobing fluorescence."

Risk Assessment

Mom waves hello goodbye from a high hospital
room like the cell of an actuarial table:
Sister's born and tallied to share our risk,
the needle of grandma's Singer stuttering stitching,

piecing together our lives of patches and fractions.
Half-aware of morbidity, mortality,
we live in an aura of life expectancy
(though I die a death or two from humiliation).

I jink in dodgeball at recess, in class wave an arm
as answers are reaped. I learn to mouth, *I know*,
lap nectar spurs in the future's wide-ruled meadow.
I pledge to the forager's credo: Give all for the swarm.

But a random fart will torpedo the data pattern
as my underselves blurt scorn for what's underwritten.

Pimp Shoes

Did I mean to stalk the streets in cothurni? Shit, no.
I just failed to foresee the precarious vaudeville wobble
as the head with its chorus surveys what's unsteady below,
its kibitzing voices tsk-tsking a double hobble

(*another fine mess chalked up to clueless hubris*),
hands groping for balance but looking as if I would break
into patter-song: *oh hamartia*, convivial riff.
And a fool might truly say, *he's a dupe of the Fate*

that dogs the consumer, scammed with apotheosis
and the heady allure of a glowing ocher toe cap.
But watch me teeter in glory, a pimp Oedipus,
eyes level with second-floor shops for Pedi-Mani.

Elevation was my downfall, catastrophe
my rise. And my marrow's red honey—fear, pity.

Brand Magpie

If a large and expanding customer base were your target,
thwarted love *would merit a big share of voice.*
But, face it, you compete in a niche market
where brand personality will motivate choice.

Rejuvenate your struggling brand with a platform:
mission, vision, values, image. Magpie
captures the out-take. You're "mocketing" a swarm
of chatter—recycle the obsolescent "I."

Belly-voice huckster, I'm not a chorus, just one
lovesick over a haughty reader who shops
for items like the Canzoni Towel Collection®
at outlets for bed, bath, and poetic products.

Leverage the omens, "Just one's for sorrow," be bold
and multiply, "Seven is for a secret untold."

You

always had what I lacked and could be anyone,
but still I knew that you were always you—
otherness was your sterling qualification
and your glossy skin, a cv that glowed like dew,

proclaimed that you were braver, wiser, stronger,
and so I hedged, taking a long position:
me now, but delivery of you in the future,
trades that enhanced my market situation.

You had the goods and I had you on call,
but I could always opt out with a put
and on this basis I sold—remarkable—
myself to myself. But reader, we've reached the limit...

I've cornered the market on me, but I'll sell you the shimmer.
When the bubble has burst, volatility is tender.

Our Village

Our village is always on the verge of the Season.
The wide-girthed elms like professors at a cocktail
party, rustle loftily, in detail,
as if the lack of advent had its reasons.

In this overture, even the dirt is a dizzy prop,
whizzed from place to place by landscapers' pick-ups,
and the retail epiphany, the light so fervent
in a shop window, might just be a beam from a batten.

Poised before a mansion whose front is a flat,
a clutch of girls—early audience or late crew?—
their calves backlit beside the stems of tulips,
wait. He strolls by in the moment of a hat.

On the empty porch, a jar aglitter with fireflies—
legends of the coming Season ignite.

Illumined Century

The Booth Room at The Players

Truth was the lightning-stroke of the histrionic
gesture: the illumined century, slippers
et al—now rotting—gloriously consigned
to us by the great tragedian, who penned

(cast as his brother's keeper) an apology
to the nation. Death-mask of Terry (... *monumental
alabaster*), bust of the Bard. The empty
brass bed and limned above the east room's portal

(how small the bed, how strange to live under inscriptions!)
Sancho blessing the Author of sleep's intermissions.
Edwina's chaise: "[Lightning, blackout, eloquence]
Don't let father die in the dark!" *The rest*

is silence. Mildew, windows on night's park
and this nutshell illusion kindled by the dark.

Imitation Games

I think continually of those at a party
inside my mind, when all my guests have gone
into another room, and I must question
them blindly, passing in slips of paper, and they

wittily pelt me with tricky, subtle
trivia—*hottest full rips of hip-hop?, the pets
who loved you best?, or your favorite Sidney sonnet?*
("With how sad steps...") —to see if we can tell

who's real and male or female. Of course, the twist
is that we must always be other: Provocative
A.L.I.C.E., Eliza, dark ladies, this party of one
and many is an unceasing interrogation.

But O Tiresias, Turing, will blood still buy
prophecy in a system that's text-only?

Dear Auditor

This is to certify that I celebrate
myself and sing myself, per the contract,
in conformance with your estimate
of me, and in compliance with best practices.

Although the review has revealed my overage
and disclosed that random centers resist controls,
I am large and contain multitudes to manage
our systems, so I may loaf and invite my soul.

I do not snivel, I make these representations:
I affirm my fictitious business name is Kosmos
and find I incorporate gneiss, coal, long-threaded moss
and proclaim from the rooftops my bonus—in vain, allegations.

Are the figures elusive? Persist in your review.
The sum of me stops somewhere, waiting for you.

Warranty and Envoy

This sonnet is ultra-modern, rhetoric-free
during normal use, nor will it drip
with maudlin emotion. Its verbal polish resists
blurring, garbling, incoherency.

That understood, consumer, why this waste
of shame to possess you, this expense, this haste
as I see you shimmer, original purchaser,
mirrored in damaged words whose cost we may cover.

This warranty proposes a joy that turns
to woe as installation fumbles and labor
bungles repair. So, these parts are in lieu
of the all we were each promised: I, you.

All other guarantees, expressed or implied
(though you *may* have other rights), are null and void.

PRAISE FOR PHILIP FRIED'S
Big Men Speaking to Little Men
(Salmon, 2006)

Philip Fried, a New York based poet, editor of *The Manhattan Review,* and, bless him, "poetry advocate," according to the blurb, is also an experienced writer at the top of his game. . . . *Big Men Speaking to Little Men* is his third collection and there is much to admire here. . . . He reminds me of Ashbery in his variousness, his excitability, his jump-cut, multifarious images, but without Ashbery's exquisiteness and with fewer deliberate abstractions. This is urban and urbane poetry, it is succinct and quick. . . .

—AMY WACK, *POETRY LONDON*

"Do I not bleed? Do I not commute?" asks Fried, who goes on to say, "my many selves travel." His layered third collection superimposes the imaginary on the actual, the sacred on the profane, and the comic on the tragic in 54 shapely poems that follow these traveling selves. From India to the Jersey Shore, from an airport's imagined saint—"Our Lady of Every Destination"—to Victor Hugo playing hopscotch, Fried, who is the founding editor of *The Manhattan Review*, attempts to transform "the world's infantile, satisfied babble" into something legible. A bit of fool's gold becomes a way to consider "the false / facet of self that would sell"; an old drive-in theater's speaker stands become "graves in the heart's Arlington." There is no parsing the real from the surreal in these poems, as when people talking on mobile phones while looking at Rodin's sculptures suddenly speak across space and time with the dead, and a statue's penis is mistaken for a handset. Fried (*Quantum Genesis,* 1997) has to inhabit these other selves in order to find what he's looking for: "an elsewhere interwoven / with here and everlastingly now."

—PUBLISHERS WEEKLY (On-line)

. . .This poetry is smart, pensive, with sometimes a wistful sadness underneath: "I was born / As a dizzily spinning disc of black shellac, / Died as fleeing tracks in an infinite snowfield" ("My Life in Film"). The ego is withheld—or sublimated into thought. For there is a quiet force in the way these poems sustain a progression. Ideas emerge from one image and glide to another, altering in flight. "Empty/Waiter" opens with a speaker gripping a ticket atop the Eiffel Tower, moves to Baudelaire's cenotaph (numinous site for a poet), where a metro ticket props up a rose. Then on to a restaurant, which dissolves, leaving waiter and speaker, who "will give him my orders from the unwritten, infinitesimal / menu, trusting that he will take but never fulfill / any as he glides them slowly in air with the Tai / Chi exercise form called Empty // Waiter."

In *Differences* (Alabama, 2004), Marjorie Perloff spoke of how U.S. poetry lost its edge after the Vietnam War, especially when weighed in the scales of abstract and omnivorous critical schemes: "In the seventies . . . the production of poetry had become a kind of bland cottage industry, designed for those whose intellect was not up to reading Barthes or Foucault or Kristeva." Whether the past tense or the present perfect should denote that situation is for others to say. However, Fried's poems incorporate the thought of our time without weakening the elusive throb of poetry. . . .

—LEM COLEY, *AMERICAN BOOK REVIEW*

. . . The book ends with "Exit from *Uncle Vanya*," a poem set in the late winter of 2003— during the run-up to the Iraq War. Leaving a performance of Chekhov at the Brooklyn Academy of Music, the speaker reluctantly, yet with a sense of duty to face the times in which he happens to live, leaves the conjured world of old Russia to reenter "life in the new / empire, and the prospect of war." These lines, grave and dignified, bring the reader face to face with tangible experience. So many contemporary poems seek to charm us, to convince us to be on their side, to make us like them. Without resorting to a blustering plain speech, Fried's poems make us come to them. This is not because they lure or compel, but because they transmit on the middle frequencies of what Keats called "the viewless wings of poesy." Fried, as editor of *The Manhattan Review*, has graciously foregrounded the poetry of others over his own work, which now calls us to rigorously attend to it.

—NICHOLAS BIRNS, *BARROW STREET*

Let me start off with the title, *Big Men Speaking to Little Men.* What Fried has done here is to take ALL-HISTORY, ALL-ART, ALL LITERATURE and somehow relate it to our Yankee-Gringo Here and Now. So get ready for a long swim in the ocean of World Culture. And because of Fried's larger cultural overview, his comments on the contemporary scene have a lot more impact and power. . . .

—*Hugh Fox, IBBETSON UPDATE* (On-line)